You Make My Heart Sing

Written by
Dr. Morgan Walls

Illustrated by
Stephanie Hider

Copyright © 2021 Little Sparkles Publishing
All rights reserved. No part of this book may be reproduced or transmitted in any form or by any means, electronic or mechanical, including photocopying, recording, or by any information storage and retrieval system, without written permission from the publisher, except in the case of brief quotations embodied in critical reviews and certain other noncommercial uses permitted by copyright law.

Illustrations by Stephanie Hider
Layout by Praise Saflor

Library of Congress Control Number: 2021913970

ISBN: 978-1-7375669-2-2 (Hardcover)
978-1-7375669-0-8 (Softcover)
978-1-7375669-1-5 (Ebook)

For my parents, whose love inspired this story.
To my husband, who makes my heart sing.

One day, a long time ago,
a little thought came to me.

That thought grew
    into a special dream,
        wondering what could be.

That dream turned into a special prayer
that I would whisper every night,

and I'd close my eyes to go to sleep,
but the picture was still in sight.

I imagined the good things
that you would bring
and pictured how
you would make my heart sing.

And then, one day,
I'm glad to say,
my special dream came true.
"What was that dream?"
you ask me.

It was you, my child,
	with hands so small they fit
		like a puzzle piece in mine.

With the smallest feet,
 and the littlest toes, I'd tickle,
  as you wiggle and giggle.

Each day my heart grows bigger
with the joy and light you bring,

and just as I dreamed it would,
your smile makes my heart sing.

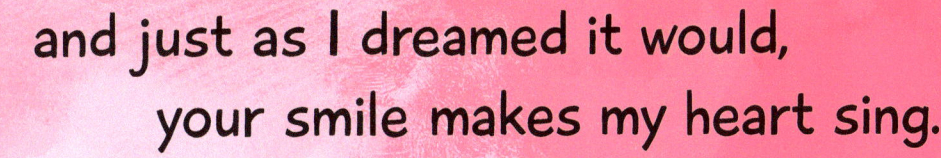

My heart sings a song of happiness and love.
If you listen closely you may hear it singing
"thank you" to God above.

Now I know your hands
will not always be small
and I love watching you grow.

But no matter how big you get through the years,

there is something
 I want you to know.

So I'll tell you no matter how old you are,
you will always find this to be true:
I'll treasure every chance I get
to say that I love you.

About the Author

Dr. Morgan Walls, MD, MS is a board-certified general pediatrician, researcher, and author. Dr. Walls has had a love for children's books since a young age, yet it was in her role as a pediatrician when she learned the significant impact that early reading has on child development. Her first book, *You Make My Heart Sing*, was inspired by her desire to foster the positive child development that occurs through parental expression of love and shared reading experiences. She resides in North Carolina where she enjoys spending time with her husband, family, and friends.

www.ingramcontent.com/pod-product-compliance
Lightning Source LLC
Chambersburg PA
CBHW041703160426
43209CB00017B/1734